IT WAS WRITTEN

It was written

Aldivan Torres

aldivan teixeira torres

CONTENTS

1 - 1

1

It was written
Aldivan Torres
It was written

Author: Aldivan Torres
2020- Aldivan Torres
All rights reserved.

This book, including all its parts, is copyrighted and cannot be reproduced without the permission of the author, resold or transferred.

Aldivan Torres, born in Brazil, is a writer consolidated in several genres. So far, the titles have been published in dozens of languages. From an early age, he was always a lover of the art of writing, having consolidated a professional career from the second half of 2013. He hopes, with his writings, to contribute to international culture, awakening the pleasure of reading in those who do not have the habit. Your mission is to win the hearts of each of your readers. In addition to literature, its main amusements are music, travel, friends, family, and the pleasure of life itself. "For literature, equality, fraternity, justice, dignity, and honor of the human being always" is its motto.

Dedication and Acknowledgments

I dedicate this work to my mother, to my family, to my readers, to my followers and admirers. I would be nothing without you. Furthermore, I especially dedicate this work to everyone who pursues their dreams.

I thank God first of all, my relatives and myself for always believing in my potential. I'll go even further.

"In his heart man plans his way, but the Lord determines his steps."

Proverbs 16:9

Introducing

"It was written" is a work based on real facts. Inspired by the film of the same name, it shows the trajectory of a boy born in the backwoods of the Brazilian northeast in a family of farmers. Facing all kinds of adversity, he grew up hoping to fulfill his dreams. The young man is an artist in his highest degree of completeness: Writer, poet, composer, and screenwriter.

The greatest lesson the book brings is that of perseverance. There is no difficult or impossible dream to fulfill. Just have the appropriate elements and know how to properly plan the stages of the project. I wish that this book will inspire many young people to keep fighting for their dreams. You have to have faith in your potential. A hug to all and good reading!

The Author

Scene 1- Kitchen

Father

What do we have to eat today, woman?

Mother

Same old thing.

Father

That's good. At least we have food today.

Divine

Father, could you buy bread for me?

Father

We have no money, Divine.

Divine
But I wanted so badly to eat bread.

Father
So, work! Today you will help me in the plantation. I promise that if you work well, I'll buy the bread for you.

Divine
What about my study day? I'll lose?

Father
Do you want to eat? Remember that the rewards come from efforts.

Divine
All right, I'm going to work!

Scene 2 — Climbing the Saw

Divine
Father, what must I do to become a great man?

Father
Firstly, study. Then use that knowledge for your goals and dreams. I want you to know, my son, that nothing will be achieved without effort or work. You will have to fight a lot if you want to win because you were born in a hostile environment of poverty and injustice as is the Brazilian Northeast. I ask you not to despair in difficult times. God is with you.

Divine
I promise to fight, my father. I also count on your understanding when I need it.

Father
I will understand. But I beg you not to embarrass me in front of society.

Divine
What do you mean?

Father

You are still a child to understand this. But society is a set of rules. To be respected, we have to follow her standards.

Divine

Forgive me, Father, but I do not agree. I have my values and opinions. To hell with society if it goes against your rules. I just want to be happy!

Father

So be it so! Get ready for a tough battle!

Divine

I am minimal, but I am already a great warrior! I will fight, and I promise you that I won't lose.

Scene 3- In the Fields

Father

I'll teach you how to plant, my son. In each pit, place three bean seed and four corn seed.

Divine

Understood, father.

Divine

I'm tired, Dad!

Father

We're done, son! Let's go home!

Divine

I'm just a wreck! I'm not feeling well!

Father

Every first time is like this! Then it gets better!

Divine

I hope so!

Scene 4- In the living room of the house

Father

Son, I'm going out to buy food!

Divine

All right, Dad!

Mother

Divine is lying in the room with a high fever. What'd you do with him?

Father

Nothing! We only work today on the fields!

Mother

My love, think it over! Are not you being tough on him?

Father

Why do you say that?

Mother

It is clear that this boy was not born to country life. It is too fragile to endure a toil in the field. Look what you did to him: Missed class and is still sick. Pleased?

Father

I did not know that was going to happen. What do you suggest?

Mother

He is a boy very dedicated to studies. I believe that can win in life because he has a lot of willpower. How about giving him a chance? A chance we didn't have.

Father

You're right. Divine deserves this chance. I'll grant. But here on the place he would never have opportunities. I'll send him to stay with my cousin Abel in town.

Mother

Great idea. It's a good thing you reflected!

Scene 5- In the living room of the house

Divine

I'm going to town. I appreciate the opportunity. As soon as I get money, I'll send it to you.

Mother

Do not worry about it now. Focus on your studies. I still want to see you, a great man.

Divine

That's right, Mom! I promise you will see!
Father
Obey your cousin Abel. Study hard and never cease to write for us. Come and visit us when you can.
Divine
All right, Dad! I'll behave well.
Father
Thanks, son.
Scene 6 — In the car
Divine
Can you go faster, driver?
Driver
Young people are really impatient. This is going nowhere.
Divine
I was born this way. I am the fruit of these backwoods of my God, where the poor have no time. I was born with hunger, hatred, and thirst for justice. Why so much inequality in the world? Why so much falsehood, lies and greed? We have not come all from the dust and to the dust we will return? We are not the same before God? That is why, I do not understand the inequalities of this world.
Driver
You're too young to understand. But I'll teach you something. The one in charge in this world is pride and money. The poor finances the benefits of the rich with their labor. This generates inequality. People are lying to win. The honest ones almost always lose because what counts are to be smart. Although we are dust, many people feel superior because they are beautiful, rich, or famous. When the man is upper-class simply ignores the existence of the lower class.
Divine
Exact. I am the opposite of what others are. I am a being without prejudice, with much disposition and dreams. I do not

give up easily. I'm leaving my parents' house for the first time. I'm going to live with my cousin. I want to study and be someone in life.

Driver

That. Just don't forget us, poor country people, also dreamers.

Divine

I promise here before you. Even if I win the world, I cannot change. I'll remain the little country people of the Brazilian Northeast. Nothing will make me lose my essence. If there was, I would not be the son of God.

Driver

A strong word. Where did you get that, boy?

Divine

My entities named me like this. The human being is the union of two parts, Yin and Yang. Miraculously, I am only good that gave me predicates to that name.

Driver

Stop lecturing, boy.

Divine

The northeast is forgotten by the authorities, but it's never been forgotten by God. Believes it and you will have found the right path.

Driver

It's ok! Let me concentrate a little now! Take a rest!

Divine

Yes sir! I'm in your good hands.

Scene 7- In the entrance of the house of the cousin

Driver

We're here, boy! Now it's up to you. Follow your dreams, and we'll all be cheering for you.

Divine

Thank you, friend, here is your payment! Everything you'd want for me; I also wish for you.

Driver

This money will help me a lot. In times of unemployment, anything is good. God bless you!

Divine

Amen! To us all!

Scene 8- In Cousin's living Room

Divine

Good morning, everyone, I come from the place of hope. My name is Divine, which means little dreamer.

Abel

My cousin's son! Welcome! Make yourself at home!

Daniel

My name is Daniel, Abel is my father. In me, you have the support you need.

Divine

Thank you, all! How can I contribute to a good relationship between us?

Rosane

It has to be an obedient, polite and helpful boy.

Daniel

You have to be reasonable in your actions, knowing your limits.

Abel

You have to be understanding and respect me as the head of the house. You have to work to pay your expenses. Always remember that you are not at your parents' house. Here everyone has their responsibility.

Divine

I am aware of everything I have to do and how to behave. I promise to be useful to everyone. On the other hand, I also want respect. I left my parents' house decided to win. Tell me, Mr. Abel, when do I start?

Abel

You are in heaven! For me, you can start now. I want you to clean the house in general, take care of the dirty bathrooms, clean the rooms, and prepare the lunch. In the afternoon, give a bath on my horse and go for a walk with my dog. At night, you can finally study because I've already enrolled you in the neighborhood school.

Divine

All right, cousin! You thought of everything.

Rosane

That! We think of the good and our convenience! I'll swing by my sister's house while you work. I know the house will be in good hands.

Daniel

I'm going to my friend's house play video game. I'm glad we have you to help us, Divine.

Abel

I'm going to the company to take care of some issues, and then I'll come back. I come to check the quality of your work. I have a great concern about the quality of services.

Divine

Everyone goes with God. I will be fine! Working has never made me afraid. I'll do my best.

Rosane

Great, dear!

Scene 9- In the hallway

Divine

Is a great house! Now I see that it will not be easy to keep what I promised! Even if it's hard, I cannot give up now! My family depends on my effort to survive! I cannot disappoint them. All the obstacles give me the strength to continue. Regardless of the result, I consider myself a winner.

Divine

I finished cleaning! Now I'm going to prepare lunch.

Scene 10- In the kitchen

Divine

I do not have much experience with food! Will I be able to prepare something good?

Divine

As my mother says, for food to be good it has to be made with love. This I have plenty of!

Abel

Divine, are you ready?

Divine

Yes, I finished it now.

Abel

I need your help. Let's go to the room!

Divine

It's ok!

Scene 11- In Cousin's Room

Abel

You are quite handsome, Divine! I'll teach you something!

Divine

Is it good or bad?

Abel

It's transformer!

Abel rape Divine

Divine

Monster! Why did you hurt me like this? It looks like I even liked it!

Abel

That means you're homosexual.

Divine

What is homosexual?

Abel

People who like the same sex. Thank me for discovering yourself.

Divine

I do not know if I hate you or thank you! The future will tell!

Abel

Do not tell anyone. Otherwise, I'll kill you!

Divine

Save my life! I still want to win in life.

Abel

So be tactful.

Divine

I promise I will.

Scene 12- In the kitchen

Rosane

This is crap! You do not know how to cook, Divine?

Divine

I did my best!

Rosane

I have already seen that you do not have much talent. You make me cook. Have you thought about the damage you're going to cause to my nails? I dismissed the maid when I heard you was coming.

Divine

I'm so sorry! Please forgive me and let me continue in this house.

Rosane

What do you think, Abel?

Abel

He did a great cleaning on the house. In addition, is careful and hardworking. Therefore, deserve a chance!

Daniel

That, mother, give him a chance! With whom would I vent? With Whom I would fight or imply?

Rosane

It's ok. I've already seen that I have a heart of gold for being able to endure this starvation here at home. This is the family from your father! It only gives me trouble.

Abel

There is no perfect family, woman! Think of it as an act of charity.

Rosane

Now tell me, fool, who pities us when we're in the gutter? We can only count on ourselves.

Divine

When I decided to come here, I came to collaborate. I helped for my manner with my effort. God knows how important it is for me to study. But if I'm being a burden on everyone, I can leave.

Abel

Do not say it Divine, I promised your father. Do not listen to others. Remember that I am the boss here.

Divine

Thanks, cousin.

Daniel

Every family is like that, Divine. My mother and I do not have easy temperament. But you get used to it in time. In life we get used to everything, isn't it?

Divine

Not always, Daniel. Sometimes circumstances lead us to drastic decisions. Although we are at the beginning of everything.

Daniel

Yes, heaven or hell started for you.

Abel

Divine, go and take care of your other obligations. See you later.

Divine

It's ok! I'm going!

Scene 13- In front of the cousin's house

Divine

I already took the dog for a walk and I already bathed the horse. I fulfilled my obligations of the afternoon. How am I going to study exhausted?

Angel

Strength, Divine. I'm with you at all times.

Divine

Who are you?

Angel

I'm your guardian angel. From now on, we will always be in connection.

Divine

What is a guardian angel?

Angel

I am your spiritual protector. I take your requests to God and I protect you from all evil.

Divine

I'm very grateful for that. What do you tell me of me being in the house of strangers?

Angel

This will generate learning for you. But always remember your warrior spirit, you are like the lion of David who does not submit to anyone.

Divine

I know that. I am in a difficult and confusing moment. My dreams are being run over. I need to fight, but the current is forceful.

Angel

I will fight with you. Your God is stronger than the current. Follow your intuition always.

Divine

I'll try. Something tells me to move on and face the situation. I trust in victory.

Angel

Very well. See you later.

Divine

See you later.

Scene 14- In the classroom

Teacher

Good night, everyone. I hope everyone is well. I see there's a newbie in the classroom. What is your name?

Divine

My name is Divine. I come from the interior with many guts. I want to study and be someone in life.

Student

Divine, this is the name of a faggot.

Divine

I do not know what you mean. But I really like my name.

Student

So, you're openly faggot. Isn't it people?

The others

Faggot!

Shirley

Leave him alone, you wankers! Do not mind them, Divine. They're just unloved!

Divine

Thank you for defending me. You're beautiful and kind!

Shirley

You too! Receive my gift! These sweets I made it myself!

Divine

Thank you! What's your name?

Shirley

Shirley. Much pleasure!

Divine

The pleasure is all mine!

Teacher

How much is the square root of forty-nine?

Student

twenty-five!

Another student

Ten!

Divine

Ten!

Teacher

Congratulations, Divine! You're smart for your age!

Divine

Thank you, teacher!

Student

That was just luck!

Divine

It was competence! I've been studying a long time! Follow my example!

Student

God forbids! I do not want to be faggot! I'm a male!

Teacher

Focus, Guys! Let's study!

Scene 15 — Cousin's living Room

Abel

How was your study day?

Divine

Very helpful despite the difficulties. I really liked it! I'm very hopeful.

Abel

How nice! I'm happy for you!

Rosane

What do you carry in the bag, Divine?

Divine

Some candy that a girl gave me as a gift.

Daniel

I love candy! Can I stay with them, Mom?

Rosane

Of course, son! I also love sweets!

Divine

What? The gift is mine!

Abel

Be generous, Divine! Remember that you are not in your home. Everything that comes here is our property.

Divine

It's ok! Stay with the candy! At least I will not have diabetes!

Rosane

Nor will we have diabetes, muggle. Let's split between us. Thank you for understanding! Keep being kind! A good evening!

Divine

A great night!

Scene 16- In the Room

Divine

I'm completely exhausted and dizzy! When I left the place, I didn't imagine that it was so difficult. I feel powerless in the face of obstacles. I am moved only by faith!

Angel

That! You have a lot of faith! God is with you, Divine!

Divine

I'm glad you're here. You're the only friend I have.

Angel

I'm always with you. I will strengthen your faith in the walk. Your trajectory is long!

Divine

Long and full of suffering? How will I endure it? I can't even have my thing in this house.

Angel

You are free to make decisions! Wherever you go, you will face difficulties. But each experience will strengthen your character and your strength.

Divine

Am I so small? I can make decisions? And my family?

Angel

At this point, you only depend on your strengths. Just continue with determination, guts, and courage!

Divine

You're right! I dislike this house. I want to know and face the world.

Angel

Big idea! I will be with you!

Divine

Thank you, my friend,

Scene 17- In the Living Room

Divine

The great day has come! I'm leaving this house!

Rosane

What is it, foolish boy?

Divine

That's what you heard, witch! I'm very close to my freedom.

Rosane

You will not survive! The world outside is much worse than you think.

Divine

I'm ready! I'm tired of being your doormat, of not having my freedom or my things. Furthermore, I grew up, and now I want my space.

Daniel

What am I going to tell your parents? Don't you think about your family?

Divine

I'm sure they would support my decision. Anyway, in this house I will never be happy. I need to try new paths in my trajectory. I need to find myself.

Abel

I'm proud of your determination. You are admirable. It remains for me to wish you good luck and ask forgiveness for my failures.

Divine

Thanks for the stay for this time. I do not want nor can holding grievances and resentment anyone's because I need to be happy. Be in peace!

Scene 18- In the street

Divine

I'm walking for hours without a destination. What do I do, my God?

Street Woman

I see you're lost. What a fine-looking boy like you do around here?

Divine

I left my cousin's house.

Street Woman

Because you left?

Divine

I was not happy there. I was everyone's doormat. Furthermore, I lived horrible days, months, and years in the company of petty people. Furthermore, I suffered atrocities.

Street Woman

Poor little thing! I imagine your suffering. I admire your courage to leave a house. But have you ever thought that may have been a wrong decision? What makes you believe that on the street you'll get something better?

Divine

Honestly, I do not know what awaits me in this new phase of my life. But I'm not afraid. If I survived more than a decade of humiliation, I can conquer everything. I'll still be the pride of my family!

Street Woman

You are already the pride of your family. Make sure of that. Look, I'm an administrator of this place. Stay here with me and I will protect you. Living in the streets is extremely dangerous for innocent young people like you.

Divine

Thank you very much. God bless you! I'm ready to fight and win again. What is your name?

Street Woman

My name is Katherine and you?

Divine

My name is Divine. I am also known as the son of God, Seer and little dreamer.

Street Woman

Welcome, son of God, who honors.

Divine

The pleasure is mine.

Scene 19- Working as a deliverer

Divine

Good morning, do you want some help, ma'am?

Woman

Yes, young man. Could you take my bags? They are very heavy.

Divine

Of course, yes. I am at your disposal. Where are we going?

Woman

To my house. Follow me!

Divine

It's ok!

Woman

What's your name, handsome young man?

Divine

Call me Divine. And you?

Woman

I'm Kassandra. What a beautiful name. Where do you live?

Divine

I'm a homeless. I've been trying to survive with these little jobs for a while.

Woman

You are admirable. Now you're making me curious. Could you tell me a bit about your story?

Divine

Yes, of course, with pleasure. I was born in the interior, into a family of farmers. From an early age, I learned to value work and struggle. Even living with the drought, hunger, and indifference of the authorities, I never stopped dreaming. My goal was always to study and become a good man. I want to win with my strength. Since I did not have options to study in the countryside, I was sent to my cousin's house in this city. That's where I lived a real hell. In addition to work as a slave, I was humiliated at all times. To have a chance to win, I swallowed the crying and kept fighting. It was more than a decade of constant suffering and sorrow where I was that's doormat. That's why I prefer to live on the streets. I keep on going with my dreams without disturbing anyone. I do not know when I will win, but victory is certain and promised by my God. This glorious being is called Jesus. He is the father of the poor and forgotten by the world.

Woman

What an impressive story. What is your main dream?

Divine

I want to be a filmmaker. I want to tell my story and the story of other people through the movie screens. Furthermore, I see in this art a fantastic thing: The staging of various realities. Furthermore, I often cry with moving and dramatic scenes. The issue of overcoming obstacles, combating injustice, the abuse of cruel people, confronting unequal among others generate striking stories. This is what I want to do: Create stories.

Woman

It is a noble dream but rather difficult. Do you think it is easy to make movies in a Third World country where the financing of the works depends almost exclusively on government money? Have you thought about competing with foreign cinema? The competition is too brutal and the risk of failure is too great.

Divine

I already know all this, but I do not give up. Obstacles were made to be overcome. If I'm still alive after all I've suffered, there's a bigger plan in my life. I will be David facing Goliath without fear of losing. Just trying I'm already a winner.

Woman

His strength is admirable and enviable. If I thought like you, I had not given up so young.

Divine

What was his dream?

Woman

My dream was to be a professional writer. But after a decade of failures, I gave up. I ended up retiring as a primary school teacher.

Divine

I did not want to fail. Furthermore, I wanted to make a difference. Furthermore, I wanted one day to be at the Oscars, getting a prize for my country. Furthermore, I did not want this prize out of vanity, I just wanted to show the world that when we believe in dreams and fight for them, victory is possible.

Woman

You will win. I want to live to see that day and applaud you on your feet. I believe in your conquest of the world!

Divine

May God hear you! I do not know if I am worthy of this grace someday, but I'll try. At the moment, I just want to survive with my jobs. That's why I ask for your generosity.

Woman

You deserve. I'll do everything in my power. Congratulations on being this young dreamer!

Divine

Thank you for the compliments. Let's move on! The weather is urgent!

Woman

You're right! Let's follow with faith!

Scene 20- Arrival at the house

Divine

Here are your things, lady! It was a pleasure to help.

Woman

Here is your payment. I've included a bonus, so you could encourage your dream.

Divine

Thank you for your kindness. God and his angels will always protect you. You were exceptional to me. It is very likely that we will not see each other again, but I will remember you throughout my career. I will call it hope.

Woman

Your hope is not vain. It is written that by tortuous ways you will find your happiness. Have hope and faith!

Divine

I have every confidence in God and in myself. Is written!

Scene 21- Proposed on the street

Man

What are you doing on the street, kid?

Divine

I've been a homeless since I left my cousin's house. There, the atmosphere was unbearable, and I preferred to live here.

Man

What a tragedy! I would like to help you. I live alone ever since my parents passed away. Do you want to live with me?

Divine

Are you certain? I will not disturb? Have a home is all I now wanted.

Man

There is no problem. Your company will lessen my loneliness. Some people have already turned down my offer because my house is haunted.

Divine

Haunted? Do you mean inhabited by spirits? Well, it must be better than living on the streets.

Man

That depends on the person. But I'll propose a test. Stay in my house for a while. This can help you develop your mediumship.

Divine

Did you realize that I am a medium?

Man

Exactly. I have sensitivity to these things. Let's go then?
Divine
Yes, let's go.
Man
Tell me a little about you.
Divine
My name is Divine. I come from the interior to the big-city searching for my dreams. I came to study and try to be a good man. And you?
Man
I am an heir from a couple of businessmen. I run my business and live here alone. In my leisure time, I try to understand the universe a little better. But tell me: What are these dreams?
Divine
Firstly, have financial stability. Subsequently, I want to become a filmmaker. I love the art of storytelling.
Man
How cool! This is really extraordinary. Can you imagine telling your story and winning a prize? What pride would you give to your family and your country?
Divine
This is still a distant dream. My current reality is work and studying. However, hope moves me to the future.
Man
Great truth! If is written, it will happen. You are quite young yet and with a future ahead.
Divine
I hope so! What about mediumship?
Man
I brought you to better understand this gift. Consider my stay a period of development and discovery. I will be your master!
Divine

What an honor! I will strive to be a good apprentice! I ran away from it my whole life, but now the time is right.

Man

Yes. Everything has its time. Welcome to my home!

Divine

Thank you very much!

Scene 22- In the room at night

Divine

Dad, I wanted to say thank you for one more day. It was another day of toil, but I feel its presence in every outdated obstacle. I feel like your child because you are my comfort and shelter. A good night!

Vampire

I will destroy you! I want to bite you!

Divine

What do you mean? Who are you?

Vampire

I am the first vampire in the world. I came to suck your blood!

Divine

You cannot because I'm good!

Angel

That's it! Leave the boy alone, monster! If not, you answer to me.

Vampire

Your luck is really be good! I'm leaving expelled by the Holy Spirit. Always thank him, boy!

Divine

I'm so glad you're here. I was afraid that monster would do me some harm.

Angel

Though evil approaches you, it will not harm you. You are the anointed of the holy father. Therefore, your name is son of God!

Divine

All glory to the Lord forever! Look, I need to talk to you. What did you think of my decision to live here?

Angel

Your ways are gradually getting more defined. If it is here, it is by divine will. Take advantage of the situation to learn more about human relationships and your gift. This will give you incredible growth.

Divine

I really need to evolve and become the man I dream and desire. I need to understand the lines of life and "be like the flowing river," completely delivered to fate. The mighty God will guide me.

Angel

Everything ends well when it ends well. I'm on your side, Divine. I am your companion in this arduous journey. We are on the road to victory.

Divine

Yes, just by the effort, we are already winners.

Angel

Stay in peace. I will always protect you.

Divine

Thank you very much!

Scene 23- In school

Divine

Kate, I wanted to tell you something.

Kate

Which is?

Divine

I like you. It's been three years that we studied together in high school and from the first moment I like you. Would you like to be my girlfriend?

Kate

Divine, what's the matter with you? I never gave you hope of dating. I want to make it clear that we are just colleagues. Besides, I already have a boyfriend.

Divine

Sorry for my statement. You always treated me so well that I thought I would have a chance. I promise I'll never bring it up again.

Kate

I'm glad you're sensible. Furthermore, I'll pretend I did not get this statement. Keep calm. My boyfriend will not know.

Divine

Thank you for that!

Scene 24- In the Living room

Divine

Good Night!

Man

Good Night! How was school, Divine?

Divine

Tragic. I just got rejected by the girl I liked.

Man

Oh my gosh! Poor thing! Sit here and unburden yourself.

Divine

I created courage and I declared myself to her. In response, I was rejected. It hurt so much, but she was caring, and we were good schoolmates.

Man

This is normal. Who has never been rejected in life? I've been several times myself. I think it's a great opportunity for reflection and cultivate self-love.

Divine

Of course, I'm happy. However, I lack affection and company. I've been studying with this girl for three years. I thought she felt the same way I do.

Man

This is sorrowful. Disappointment mistreats the soul. But you're too young. I'm sure you'll get over it and continue to have hope in finding that special someone. Believing that he exists somewhere in this world.

Divine

I feel that he exists. I want to do is get on with my normal life. Everything is in the time of God. Thanks for the comfort.

Man

For nothing!

Divine

I'm going to my room now! Good night!

Man

Good evening!

Scene 25- In the Room

Divine

I am completely alone in this world. My family is far away and cannot help me. What do I do, my God? My dreams haven't been fulfilled yet. And if I die? I'm petrified of that.

God

Are you afraid of death, Divine? Knows that death does not exist because you are an eternal being.

Divine

I know I am. But this is not enough to control the feeling that invades me when I think of it: To know that everything I have built and fought will be lost with my memory.

God

Will not be forgotten. You will live through your writings. Have you thought about how many people you will help? Your memory will not be erased for them. Remember: If there were no death there would be no life and vice versa.

Divine is crying.

God

Why are you crying? Do not cry because I will cry too.

Divine

I cannot explain, it's involuntary.

God

What do you want? You want me to do with you the same thing I did with Enoch?

Divine

How would it be?

God

I would create a hurricane and take you to the skies alive. Every day, I return to earth to get food for him. He's beautiful as you are.

Divine

No, thank you. I'm no better than my parents. I have to fulfill my mission. Besides, I would die if I went into a hurricane.

God

You would not die, man of little faith. You would not lose a single strand of your hair.

Divine remains crying

God

Stop it, your spoiled young man. Look, I promise you'll be the first to rise again in the new world. Did you know that the angels are crying so far?

Divine

Forgive me. I'm such a fool. When will the new world arrive?

God

Ten thousand years from now. If you reveal this secret, no problem. I change my plans.

Divine

Do not worry. I know how to keep secrets when it's necessary. Thank you for the words.

God

You're welcome. Well, I'll be right there. When you die, I will come to get you. Before, I reveal to you a mystery: You are one of the little particles of the Risen Christ. In my great goodness, willed that my sons were eternal. So, I turned their sacred particles into spirits. You are one of them, the most blessed. With you, I am well pleased. Isn't it surprising? While the world will mourn your loss, I will smile because you will return to my house.

Scene 26- In the Living Room

Divine

Good Morning! I want to give you some good news. Today is my first day of work on a good job.

Man

What good news! How are you feeling right now?

Divine

It's a fresh start! With the stability of the new job, I will finally be able to resume my artistic dreams.

Man

That's really good. May this work be a stepping stone to your success.

Divine

May God hear you! I will resume my work immediately. I will invest in myself so that I can reap the fruits of this work in the future.

Man

It does very well. Do your work carefully while respecting your neighbor. Remember to treat everyone professionally.

Divine

It's ok. I will do my best to perform a good role. Wish me luck.

Man
Good luck and success in your new venture.
Divine
Thank you!

Scene 27- In the Office
Divine
Good Morning. I am the new employee of this company.
Boss
Right! Welcome! I'm your boss. What can we expect from you?
Divine
You can expect commitment, dedication and hard work. I came to add talents to the team. For your part I expect understanding, respect, loyalty, honesty and justice.
Boss
What are your best qualities at work?
Divine
Teamwork, efficiency, learning ability, professionalism, isonomy and achievement of goals.
Boss
Very good! That pleases me a lot. I want to know now about your goals at this institution.
Divine
Perform well the main mission of the institution and with the salary received invest in my artistic career.
Boss
What is your art?
Divine
I am a writer, composer, poet and screenwriter. My dream of the future is to live completely from my art.
Boss
Are you sure? Here in Brazil, I do not know anyone who lives in art. I think live exclusively from art is a great madness.

Divine

You're right. But maybe I can to stand out. I also have translated works abroad. My dream is to be a screenwriter in Hollywood.

Boss

I have to agree with you. On the outside things may be easier. I'm hoping you'll achieve your dream. But how about you come back to the reality and getting to work? Is ready?

Divine

When do I start?

Boss

Right now.

Scene 28- At Work

Divine

Good morning everyone. I am the new employee of the institution. My name is Divine.

Rick

Welcome!

Ingrid

Welcome to the group. Give your best!

Brian

I'm Brian. Do you remember me? We met on the social network.

Divine

I do remember. We participated in this same selection. Welcome, too.

Brian

Thank you, Divine. I'm glad to be your new co-worker.

Divine

The pleasure is mine. You can count on me for anything.

Brian

I know that. The reciprocal is also true.

Divine

License to all. I'm going to the training what the boss recommended. See you later.

Narration

It was an intense day of struggles to the dreamy boy. Amid the initial obstacles, he came across with great doubts. However, his strength to win was greater than anything. Victory was his only alternative if he wanted to remain dreaming.

Scene 29- In the living room

Divine

Goodnight, friend. All right?

Man

All good, Divine. I was waiting for you. How was your workday?

Divine

It was a difficult day but it was fruitful. First impressions were not totally bad. It is a job like any other with advantages and disadvantages. I hope to learn fast and to stand out.

Man

Very well. Let me tell you something, Divine. Be very careful. If you to stand out, will provoke quite envy in your colleagues. This will make the workplace quite complicated.

Divine

What can I do? I have to justify my salary. I've gotten over a lot in my life. If any problem occurs, I'll know exactly how to act. Do not worry.

Man

This is inevitable. It is written: Among tortuous paths, you will find happiness. The work will give you an amazing personal growth. This can inspire you in books and scripts. Enjoy this important moment of social interaction.

Divine

Exactly! My name is overcoming! I've been through countless services, each with their learning. From peasant to official of a great institute. That was a giant leap. But I still want more. I want to win a great prize for Brazil in literature and cinema.

Man

God bless you! You are a blessed and incredible being. It deserves all the happiness in the world. What about love? How it feels?

Divine

My clairvoyance tells me that I will be happy. I do not know when nor how it will happen but I will find the right person. I still have hopes even after five rejections.

Man

You are persistent in your goals. Now, that's interesting. Five rejections. What have you done wrong, Divine?

Divine

I did not do anything wrong. God is just preserving me for the right person. I'm going to give my virginity to the loved one.

Man

Your virginity? What a beautiful attitude. This is very rare nowadays. Why did you decide that?

Divine

Today, we live in a world totally without love. Most people are prostituting herself and live-in casual relationships. They do this with fear of suffering and disappointment. I am totally the opposite of that. My ethics does not allow casual relationships. My body is sacred and your pleasure will be given to the right person.

Man

What if that person does not arrive? What are you going to do?

Divine

I'll be happy anyway. I will be happy with my work and with my charity. Furthermore, I help my family and several close people with my work.

Man

Very good! Charity erases all sin! Continue like this and you will have heaven as a reward.

Divine

This is one of my goals as well. I hope to get it!

Man

So be it!

Scene 30- At job

Divine

Good morning, everyone. I brought you a gift. I will give each co-worker a copy of my book Opposing forces. This is my first novel written in school holidays.

Brian

How cool, Divine. What did you write here? Any secrets?

Divine

In this book is my soul, my dreams and my fantastic fiction. I hope you enjoy it. Maybe you do not know me better.

Brian

I'll love it, Divine. It's always good to get to know your friends better.

Ingrid

I like books. I like spiritual and romantic literature. Thank you for the gift.

Divine

For nothing!

Rick

I also like reading, movies and theater. But no promises. After all, you're an unknown writer. I guarantee that if I do not like it, it will serve only as an ornament on my shelf.

Divine

It's all right. Read! I am open to criticism and suggestions! What I want is to learn and evolve my writing more and more.

Rick

How nice! Success!

Divine

Thank you! Now I'm going to start working! Good morning, everyone!

Scene 31- In the Office

Divine

Brian, help me out here! I'm having trouble with a task.

Brian

What is the problem?

Divine

I forgot the formatting code for the task. You remember?

Brian

I do remember. Use the enter key.

Divine

It worked! Thank you for your help! You're so kind to me.

Brian

I do no more than my obligation. Remember we're coworkers? I like to help you. You are a good person.

Divine

You're a good person, too. If you need me, you can call!

Brian

That's right! I'll call! I assure you!

Scene 32- In the bathroom

Divine

What's happening to me? My God, what happens? Your sweet and kind words touch my soul! Your physical presence makes me tremble, and I do not know how to act. This reminds me something sad in the past. Will be that the story repeat itself again? I have to be cautious. I'm going home now! Furthermore, I need to talk to my angel! Furthermore, I need your advice so effective!

Scene 33- In The room

Divine

Uriel, I need your help. Shows up!

Uriel

I'm here, sir. How can I help?

Divine

My feelings are confused. After five rejections, I have just discovered that I am loving someone.

Uriel

Great, Divine. That means you are a child of God! Love is a feeling that ennobles the soul!

Divine

I do not know my angel. I've already been so disappointed. This should not have happened. I do not deserve to suffer like the other times. You understand? Are completely crazy and impossible loves. I am homosexual and he is heterosexual. This is not Love! It's a traveling disgrace.

Uriel

Who said it would be easy? Love is inexplicable and has reasons that reason itself does not know. Now there is no turning back. It's your decision.

Divine

I'll be quiet. I'll analyze the situation and then decide. Furthermore, I intend to keep this job for a long time. But if I did not need him, I would have run away as I did at other times.

Uriel

I understand. I'm glad you're right. Keep it up and you will achieve success quickly.

Divine

Hopefully! Pray for me, angel.

Uriel

I do this every day! Nothing bad will happen to you! I promise!

Divine

I love you! Stay with me always!

Uriel

So be it!

Scene 34- At Job

Divine

Good morning, everyone. It's my birthday in seven days. It's a special date because I'm thirty years old.

Uriel

You are not going to invite us? We would like to get to know your home and your family.

Divine

My parents live in the countryside and are destitute. I haven't been able to buy a house for them. I cannot receive important people like you.

Rick

Cut the chatter, Divine. We're not your friends? What's wrong in receive us in your home? Do not worry, we are simple people.

Brian

Exact. We want to get in touch with your family and stay close to you on such a special date. This is important to me.

Divine

I apologize to everyone but this is not the time. When things improve, I promise to invite them.

Brian

Okay, then. We understand. But remember what promise is debt.

Divine

Don't worry. This moment will come.

Scene 35- In the Room

Divine

I do not know what your reaction will be, but I must try for the last time to achieve my happiness. So far, I have accumulated nine rejections. It's in God's hands.

Scene 36- In the Office

Brian

Divine, I read your message. We need to talk urgently.

Divine

All right, Brian. I'm ready!

Brian

Divine, I do not know what you think about me. I do not think you know me right. If I ever made you to think that, you would have chances with me, I beg your pardon. But you see, you're fundamentally wrong. I'm pleased with a woman. I want to marry her and have children. This is my dream. You are an extraordinary and hardworking person, a true artist that I admire. I wish you could find the right person. But that person is not me. Please do not confuse this feeling anymore. We're just coworkers. I was clear?

Divine

Obvious. Thanks for being honest with me. This hurts a lot but I will overcome. I hope we can live in peace and be good colleagues.

Brian

I wish that, too, Divine. Furthermore, I know we cannot be friends. But I want to at least have your respect.

Divine

You have my respect. Stay in peace!

Scene 37-job

Divine

The great day has come. I finished the renovation of my parents' house. That's why I invite you to have lunch at my house.

Ingrid

Great, Divine. I'm looking forward until now.
Rick
I will not be able to go. Furthermore, I have an appointment on that day. What a pity!
Divine
No problems! Maybe some other time!
Brian
It will be great! I'm very excited! Will have beer and barbecue?
Divine
Of course, yes. I'll make a nice banquet. We must celebrate this achievement, the new home of my parents.
Brian
Congratulations, mate. I'm glad to be part of this incredible story. A peasant who became a civil servant.
Divine
This is just the beginning. I still want to do my beautiful movies. I dream winning a grand prize for my country.
Brian
I do not doubt I can. You have enough strength and willingness. May the success come!
Divine
I appreciate it! All the best to you, too. I'll be waiting for you on Sunday at my house.
Ingrid
Combined! We'll be there!
Scene 38- Divine's house
Divine
Make yourself at home! The house is yours!
Boss
You have a beautiful home! I admire your concern for your family. A good son will always be a good professional.
Divine

I owe everything I am to them. My family is my foundation. Thank you for everything, my parents!

Mother

Divine was a gift that God gave me. Facing misery, he never stopped dreaming. He studied hard to achieve your goal. I believe he deserves to have success.

Father

I tried to put him in the fields, but soon I saw that he could not bear it. Furthermore, I gave him a chance and I do not regret it. Today, he is my pride!

Ingrid

You made the right decision. Your child is responsible, competent, and efficient. He justifies his salary.

Brian

He always works as a team. We help each other. His actions remind me of my late father, who was also a warrior.

Divine

What was the cause of his death?

Brian

Alzheimer's disease.

Divine

I'm so sorry. If it can comfort you, I feel that he is in heaven. Good people never die. They just changed. Happiness to your life!

Brian

Thank you, Divine. Thank you very much for the opportunity to be here. Congratulations on your achievement.

Divine

Thank you very much!

Scene 39- At Job

Rebeca

I need to talk to you. A national strike was organized. I ask everyone to participate in this important moment of our career. We need to fight for improvements.

Ingrid

You have my full support. I want salary increases, a new career structure and better working conditions.

Rick

We need to organize our claims and have enough focus. We cannot run away. Furthermore, we must win this hard battle.

Brian

I'm with you too. I know how important my participation is to this victory. And you, Divine, will you shut up?

Divine

I will not participate. I need to keep working and getting my salary. My family needs this a lot.

Rebeca

You are very selfish. How are you going to abandon us at that time?

Divine

I can help in another way.

Rebeca

There is no other way. You're running away from the battle. A strike, when it occurs, is made for all. We are the ones who are going to lose pay. And you're going to win everything without doing anything at all?

Divine

I wanted you to understand.

Brian

There is no way to support you, Divine. Forgive me but you are weak. Are you alone?

Ingrid

Do not count on me for nothing, Divine. You're a disappointment.

Divine

I'm tired. I'm going home early. Good luck to everyone on strike!

Scene 40- In the Living Room

Man

Why are you sad, Divine? Can you tell me what happened?

Divine

Things got complicated at work after the strike. I have no support from anyone else. I feel in a rough place. How I wanted to have my financial freedom to escape from there. I wanted to live from my art, but my attempts seem utterly meaningless. I send my books to publishers and I have no answer. Furthermore, I try to find a literary agent and, in these attempts, I have received more than two hundred letters of rejection. I try to convince producers to produce my scripts. However, none of them pay any attention to me. I am completely alone and unmotivated.

Man

Am sorry. Bad times serve of learning and overcoming. What do you see in your future?

Divine

I have a lot of hope. But there is a long way to go. I need to gather my strength and get over it.

Man

How about becoming a protagonist in your story? If publishers reject you, why don't you self-publish your works? If the producers do not believe in their work, how about making their productions? There is animation software on the market. This advice is also true for love affairs. How many rejections so far?

Divine

Ten rejections.

Man

Well. Try to be happy with yourself. Do not rely on anyone to be happy. Travel, practice sports, eat and dress well, anyway, enjoy life in the best way possible.

Divine

I'm already doing this. I am a pleased person. Although I feel like something is missing in me, I'm surviving. I'll get everything I want. I promise.

Man

That's the way it is. I'm here to support you. All the success in the world for you.

Divine

So be it!

Scene 41- In the Room

Divine

You will not believe what happened! I just received an invitation from a foreign producer! Finally, my story will become a movie!

Man

What a miracle! What is the name of the movie?

Divine

Is written! It tells the story of a young peasant who became a filmmaker.

Man

Wonderful. When the movie will be recorded?

Divine

Next month. I'll say goodbye to my co-workers to travel.

Man

So, go quickly before you repent. I did not say your day would come?

Divine

After ten years of trials and many awards in animation, God performed the miracle. Now is the time for farewell.

Scene 41-At work

Divine

I came to say goodbye to everyone. I'm going to travel abroad to record my movie. Thereafter, maybe I will not come back. I want to thank all the good times.

Ingrid

I do not believe it. What a miracle!

Rick

I never doubted that. One day, my day will come, too.

Brian

How is Divine, will you leave us? Have you no consideration for the good times we spent together?

Divine

I'm going after my dream as you went after yours. I also have the right to be happy. If I cannot have love, at least I'll be happy in the movies.

Brian

I understand perfectly. Good luck in your dream. I'll be rooting for you.

Divine

I know it's sincere! Bye!

Scene 42-Oscar Ceremony

News reporter

And the Oscar award this year goes to:

Is written! From Divine Torres.

Whom do you dedicate this award?

Divine

To God in the first place! My mother who begot me and my family in general! To Brian, who taught me what love is and all dreamers. I won! This Oscar is from Brazil!

News reporter

Congratulations! Very well deserved! What do you desire from now on?

Divine

I want to continue earning more prizes and seeking the love. I do not know where he is, but I know I'll find.

News reporter

Good luck, Divine. Happiness in your life.

Divine

Thank you!

Scene 43-At home

Divine

I received an email. What will it be? It's a message from Brian. Asking for a date with me. I'll meet you to find out what it's all about.

Scene 44-Beach

Divine

Thank you for have performed my dream of knowing the beach. It was so special this moment.

Brian

I wanted to be with you and to realize his dream. Congrats on the Oscar. I attended the ceremony. Do you still love me?

Divine

I love you from the first moment. But it only brought me pain because I do not fit into your dream.

Brian

I do not believe that. When there is love, there are miracles. Does this see seashell? The seawater fits in it. Why you would not fit in my dream?

Divine

Do you love me?

Brian

I always loved you, but I did not accept myself. When I realized I would lose you, I've reflected? I want you. I want to love you forever. Can you forgive me?

Divine

Love forgives all things, believes all things and endures all things. Thanks for exist. Thank you for showing me love.
Brian
My little!
Divine
My brown! Together forever!
End

www.ingramcontent.com/pod-product-compliance
Lightning Source LLC
LaVergne TN
LVHW020441080526
838202LV00055B/5301